Exploring
Space

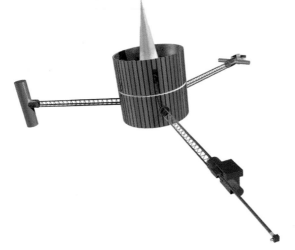

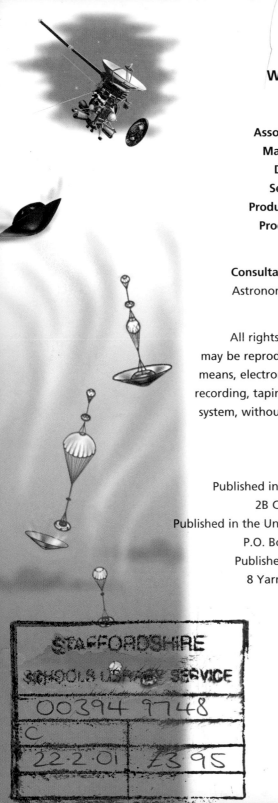

WELDON OWEN PTY LTD

Chairman: John Owen
Publisher: Sheena Coupe
Associate Publisher: Lynn Humphries
Managing Editor: Helen Bateman
Design Concept: Sue Rawkins
Senior Designer: Kylie Mulquin
Production Manager: Caroline Webber
Production Assistant: Kylie Lawson

Text: Robert Coupe
Consultant: Dr John O'Byrne, Senior Lecturer,
Astronomy Department, University of Sydney

04 03 02 01 00 99
10 9 8 7 6 5 4 3 2 1

Published in New Zealand by Shortland Publications,
2B Cawley Street, Ellerslie, Auckland.
Published in the United Kingdom by Kingscourt Publishing Limited,
P.O. Box 1427, Freepost, London W6 9BR.
Published in Australia by Shortland–Mimosa,
8 Yarra Street, Hawthorn, Victoria 3122.

Printed in Australia.
ISBN: 0-7699-0528-5

CONTENTS

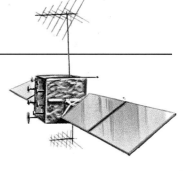

Out in Space   4

In an Observatory   6

Looking into Space   8

What Can Be Seen   10

Heading into Space   12

On the Moon   16

Sent into Orbit   18

Probing the Skies   20

Making the Journey   22

Stations in Space   24

Looking Ahead   26

Life in Space?   28

Glossary   30

Index   31

OUT IN SPACE

People have always dreamed of flying, but gravity keeps us on the ground. Over the centuries inventors have thought up all kinds of devices to overcome gravity, from hot-air balloons to the aeroplane. Once modern aircraft were invented, people began to develop ways of flying even higher—out into space. Space is the universe outside the Earth's atmosphere. About 300 kilometres above the Earth's surface, we find the upper edge of the atmosphere—that's where space begins.

VIEW FROM SPACE
This image of the area around Los Angeles was taken from a satellite orbiting the Earth. Photographs like these are used for making accurate and detailed maps.

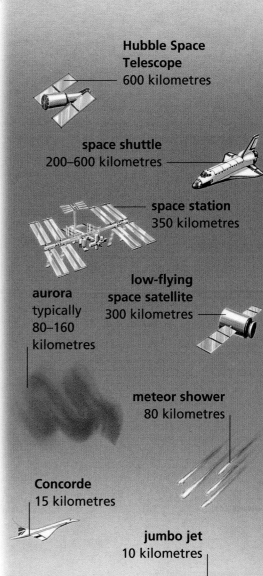

ASTRONAUT'S VIEW

This is how the Earth looks from the Moon—384,000 kilometres away. The photograph was taken on one of the journeys that astronauts made to the Moon between 1969 and 1972.

Hubble Space Telescope
600 kilometres

space shuttle
200–600 kilometres

space station
350 kilometres

aurora
typically
80–160
kilometres

low-flying space satellite
300 kilometres

meteor shower
80 kilometres

Concorde
15 kilometres

jumbo jet
10 kilometres

HOW HIGH UP?

The lowest height a satellite can safely orbit the Earth is about 300 kilometres. Here the atmosphere is very thin.

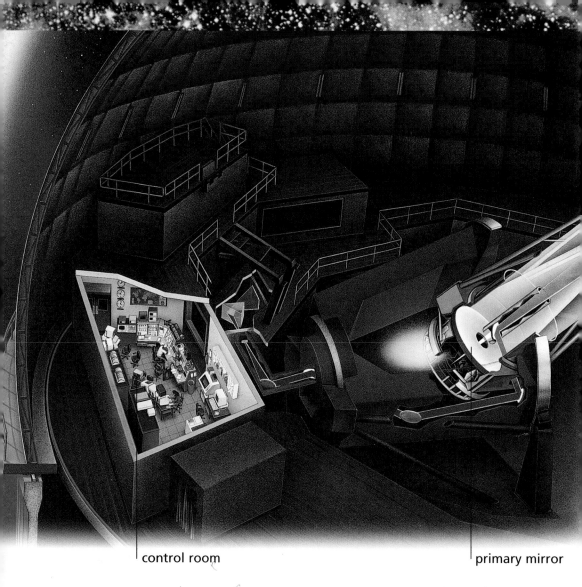

control room

primary mirror

OPENING ROOF
This observatory roof has a section that can be opened when the telescope is in use.

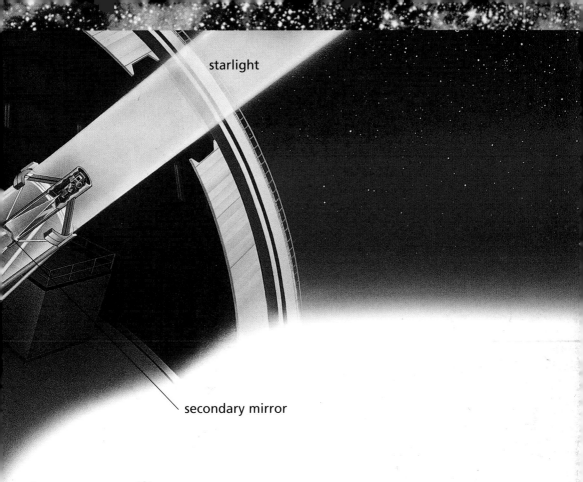

starlight

secondary mirror

IN AN OBSERVATORY

Observatories are usually built on mountains or hilltops, far away from city lights. Astronomers work at observatories using telescopes. Telescopes using starlight have mirrors to reflect light and to enlarge the images of the sky. Astronomers study these pictures on screens in a control room. The control room is the only section in an observatory viewing area that is lit—the rest is usually in darkness.

RADIO TELESCOPE
Stars and planets send out radio signals. Radio telescopes, with their large dishes, pick up these weak signals and make a radio picture of these objects.

LOOKING INTO SPACE

For thousands of years people could only observe the stars with their eyes. Then, in 1609, the Italian scientist Galileo Galilei became the first to study the sky through the magnifying lenses of a simple telescope. Sixty-two years later, the English scientist Isaac Newton invented the reflecting telescope, which uses mirrors. Since then, ever bigger and more powerful reflecting telescopes have been built. The most famous of all, the Hubble Space Telescope, is shown here orbiting the Earth.

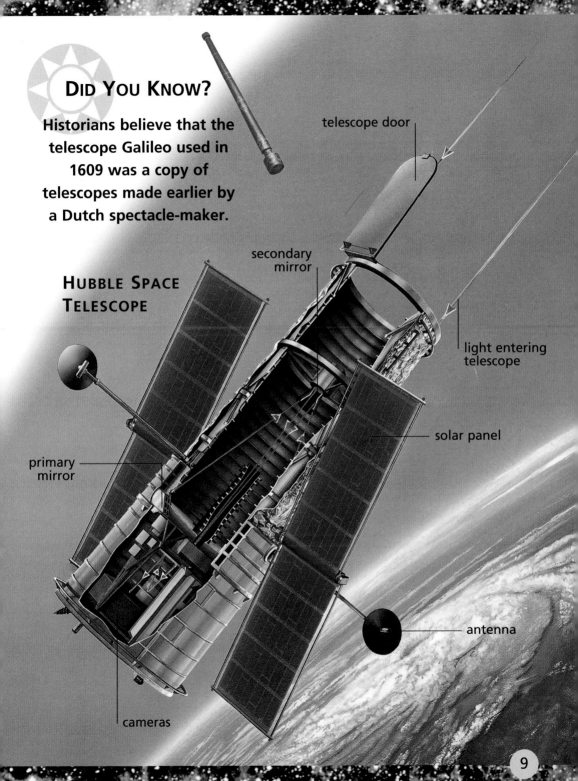

telescope door

HUBBLE SPACE TELESCOPE

secondary mirror

light entering telescope

solar panel

primary mirror

antenna

cameras

SWIRLING DISCS

Telescopes can detect the masses of stars, gas and dust that swirl around black holes. The black hole itself cannot be seen.

NEAREST LARGE NEIGHBOUR

The Andromeda galaxy is the nearest large galaxy to the Milky Way galaxy. You can see it in the night sky without using a telescope.

WHAT CAN BE SEEN

When we look into space we see billions of stars. Most of these stars live in millions of galaxies scattered across the universe. Astronomers think that many galaxies contain black holes, which sometimes form when the core of a star collapses. The core of the star shrinks to a tiny point, but its gravity can still drag in all the surrounding light and other nearby stars. The rest of the star is blown away as a supernova explosion. Giant black holes at the centre of some galaxies produce massive outpourings of energy, which we see as a brilliant point of light called a quasar.

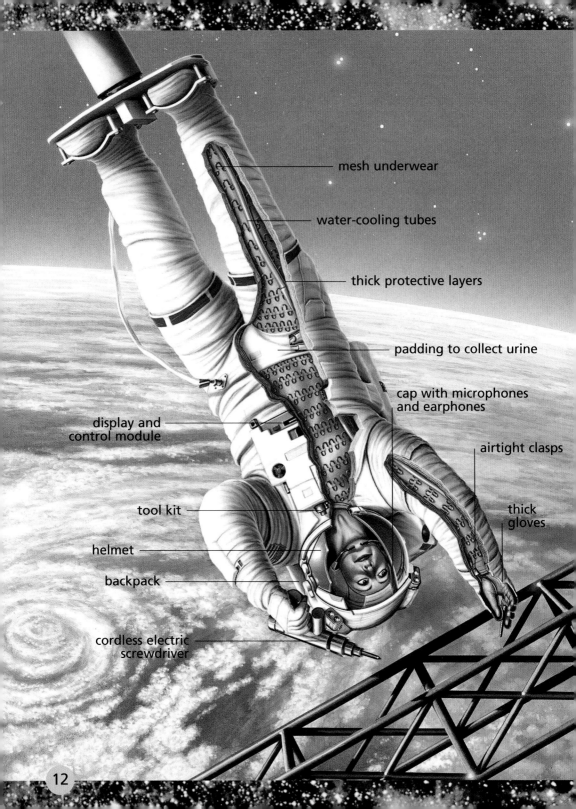

mesh underwear

water-cooling tubes

thick protective layers

padding to collect urine

cap with microphones and earphones

airtight clasps

display and control module

thick gloves

tool kit

helmet

backpack

cordless electric screwdriver

HEADING INTO SPACE

A Russian astronaut was the first human to go into space, in 1961. Now regular trips carry astronauts into space. Most astronauts stay a few days, or a week or two at most, but some live in space for much longer. Astronauts who move out of their spaceships, to do repairs or to explore their surroundings, must wear bulky suits that protect every part of their body from heat and cold. Their suits also provide air for them to breathe and keep them in touch with other astronauts. Because people feel weightless in space, these suits don't seem as heavy as they really are.

FLOATING FOOD
Inside a space shuttle an astronaut can dress normally—but eating can be a problem when you have to catch a floating sandwich!

In 1961, a Russian, Yuri Gagarin, was the first person to make a single orbit 315 kilometres above the Earth. There were many other space firsts, as Russian and United States scientists and technicians competed with each other in the "space race". In 1965, Russian astronaut Alexei Leonov made the first space walk outside a spaceship, and in 1968, three United States space explorers were the first to fly right around the Moon.

REPAIRING HUBBLE
When the Hubble Space Telescope was launched in 1990, its main mirror did not focus properly. In 1993 a crew repaired the telescope. Now it works perfectly.

SECOND WALK

In June 1965, Edward White, an American, became the second person ever to walk in space—exactly 11 weeks after Leonov.

FREE WALK

It was not until February 1984 that the first space walk was made by an astronaut who was not attached by cords to a spaceship.

On the Moon

A great event of the 20th century was the first human landing on the Moon. Millions watched on television in 1969 as Neil Armstrong took the first steps on the Moon. Over the next three years, Apollo spacecraft took 12 people to the Moon. Astronauts landed on the surface in a small craft called a lunar module, carried to the Moon by the main spaceship. During one mission, Alan Shepard used a piece of rock-collecting equipment to hit a golf ball. With less gravity and no atmosphere to slow it down, it may have been the longest golf drive ever.

LUNAR ROVER
In July 1971, astronauts used a specially designed vehicle, called a lunar rover, to explore a larger area of the Moon's surface.

In 1969, Neil Armstrong left a footprint behind on the Moon's dusty surface—and it's still there. There's no air on the Moon, so there's no wind to blow the footprint away.

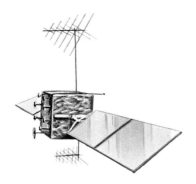

NAVIGATION SATELLITE

Navigation satellites gather information that helps ships and aircraft find out their position and plot their course.

ASTRONOMY SATELLITE

Astronomy satellites study the stars and planets and other objects in space, such as comets and meteors.

SENT INTO ORBIT

The Moon is a natural satellite of the Earth. It orbits our planet and its path is controlled by the Earth's gravity. Many artificial satellites now orbit the Earth as well, put into space by people from many nations. Different types of satellites send different information back to Earth. Weather satellites help scientists study the hole in the ozone layer over Antarctica. Space stations are also satellites, orbiting the Earth. Even without a telescope you can see satellites moving across the night sky, especially just after sunset.

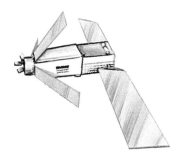

WEATHER SATELLITE

Since weather satellites have been in space, meteorologists have been able to make much more accurate weather forecasts.

COMMUNICATIONS SATELLITE

Television transmissions and long-distance phone çalls are just two of the things that rely on signals from these satellites.

SATELLITE IMAGE

Many satellites have cameras which send back images of what they can see from space. Here is a series of satellite images that show how the ozone layer above the Antarctic changed over a number of years. Ozone in the atmosphere is important because it protects the Earth from some of the Sun's harmful rays.

October 1979   October 1980   October 1981   October 1982

October 1983   October 1984   October 1985   October 1986

October 1987   October 1988   October 1989   October 1990

PROBING THE SKIES

As well as satellites, astronomers use remote-controlled robots, called probes, to study the universe. Probes can be sent to distant planets that humans cannot yet visit. They have visited every planet in our solar system except Pluto. Often they go to more than one planet during the same journey. Some probes fly past planets. Some orbit around them. Others, like the Mars Pathfinder on the right, actually land and move around the surface. So far, no probes have returned from missions into space.

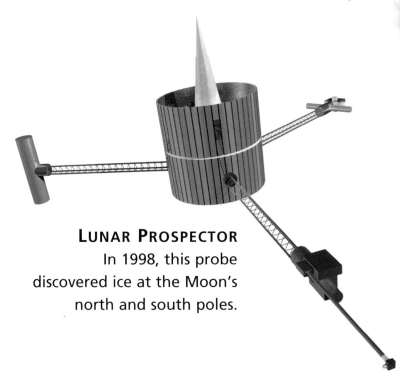

LUNAR PROSPECTOR
In 1998, this probe discovered ice at the Moon's north and south poles.

VOYAGERS

From 1979 to 1981, two Voyager probes flew to Jupiter and Saturn. Then Voyager 2 visited Uranus in 1986 and Neptune in 1989. These two probes discovered moons that nobody knew existed.

A Shuttle's Journey

Spacelab

This is a special laboratory fitted into a shuttle. Scientists use it to carry out experiments in space.

2. Rockets break away and fall back to Earth.

1. The shuttle lifts off.

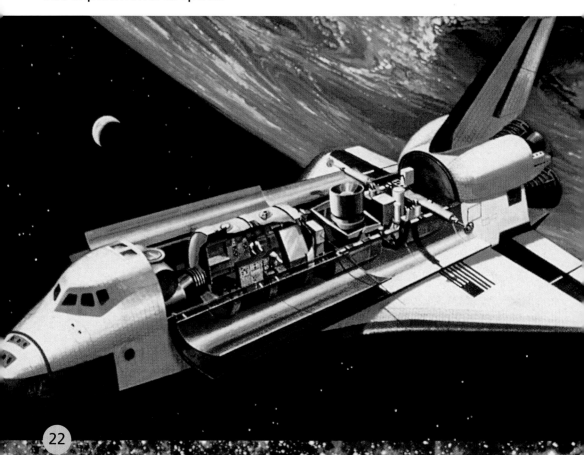

3. The large outside
fuel tank falls away.

4. The shuttle
goes into orbit.

5. It glows red as it
re-enters the atmosphere.

6. It lands on its wheels.

MAKING THE JOURNEY

Before the first space shuttle, *Columbia*, was launched in
1981, astronauts had to abandon their spacecraft in space.
They returned to Earth in a small capsule which protected
them from extreme heat as they entered the Earth's
atmosphere. Shuttles, like all the spacecraft before them,
are blasted upward through the atmosphere by powerful
rockets. When they return to Earth, shuttles land at an
airstrip. They are designed to make repeated space flights.

STATIONS IN SPACE

Space stations are large structures orbiting the Earth where people can live in space, sometimes for months at a time, conducting experiments and research on many subjects. Both Russia and the United States set up space stations in the 1970s. In 1979, the United States station, Skylab, fell towards Earth and burned up in the atmosphere. A new Russian space station, Mir, began operating in 1986 and has had visitors from many countries. Living in space for long periods without gravity can be difficult and dangerous.

LIFE ON MIR

Andrew Thomas is an Australian-born astronaut who spent five months on the Mir space station. He explained how he  had to wash with a damp cloth, because water would float away and how he slept in a sleeping bag that was tied to the wall. On Mir, they saw 16 sunrises every day.

MIR SPACE STATION

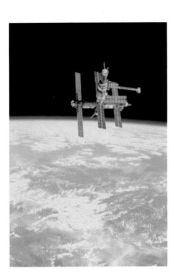

Since Mir was launched, it has been occupied almost continuously. It will be replaced by the International Space Station.

INTERNATIONAL STATION

In 2000, an international crew of three will begin living on the International Space Station. Notice in the picture above how the space shuttle will dock at the new station.

GRAVITY RESEARCH

These astronauts worked in space for two weeks, finding out about the effects of living without gravity.

CASSINI AND HUYGENS

In 2004, Cassini will release
Huygens near Titan. It will float
downward, sending pictures back
to Earth. Once it has landed it
will work for only half an hour.

A RIDE ON AN ASTEROID

A robot like the one on the right
is due to be sent to Nereus, an
asteroid near the Earth, in
2003. It will take pictures
and bring pieces of rock
back to the Earth.

Looking Ahead

Looking into the future is difficult, but astronomers will continue to unlock the universe's secrets. Many new projects are already under way. The Cassini spacecraft and its probe, Huygens, for example, are already on their way to Saturn's moon Titan. They are due to arrive there in July 2004. Further exploration will take astronauts to new destinations. Before too long, we will probably see people land on Mars.

LIFE IN SPACE?

Bulky Creatures
These might live on some planets with very high gravity.

Floating Creatures
These might live on the gas planets, such as Uranus.

The future is a mystery, and so is most of our universe. We can imagine that life exists on other planets, perhaps in distant galaxies—but at the moment we can only guess. For many years, some scientists thought that intelligent life existed on Mars. About 100 years ago, Percival Lowell, the astronomer who correctly guessed that Pluto existed, made a wrong guess about Mars. He thought that lines that astronomers saw on the surface must be canals dug by intelligent beings. We now know that Mars is uninhabited.

Stick-like Creatures
These might live where there is low gravity.

WILD GUESSES?
Here are some of the kinds of creatures that people have imagined may exist somewhere in the universe.

Walking Reptiles
These might live on planets that are like the Earth.

DID YOU KNOW?

Radio telescopes can pick up signals from distant galaxies that we cannot see through optical telescopes. If there is life out there, a radio telescope may be the first to detect it.

IMAGINARY CITY

If beings ever live on Mars, they will probably be people from Earth. Perhaps they will live and work in a city like this one.

GLOSSARY

asteroid A large piece of rock or other material that moves in orbit around the Sun.

astronomer A scientist who observes and studies the stars, planets and the rest of the universe.

atmosphere The thin layer of gases that surrounds planets such as the Earth.

galaxy A huge collection of stars, planets, gas and dust. The Milky Way is one of many millions of galaxies in the universe.

gravity A force that pulls objects towards each other. The Earth's gravity keeps us on the ground. The Sun's gravity keeps the Earth and other planets in their orbit around it.

meteorologist A person who studies the weather conditions and uses them to forecast the weather.

ozone layer A layer of gas in the Earth's atmosphere. It helps to protect plants and animals from the Sun's ultraviolet rays.

satellite Any body in space that moves in an orbit around another body.

space probe A machine that is sent from the Earth to investigate and send back information about the surface and the atmosphere of other planets and moons.

INDEX

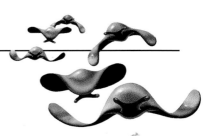

astronauts   5, 12–17, 22–25, 27
atmosphere   4–5, 16, 19, 23, 24
black holes   10, 11
galaxies   10–11, 28
gravity   4, 11, 16, 18, 24, 28
Hubble Telescope   5, 8, 9, 14
life in space   24, 25, 28–29
lunar module   16
lunar rover   16
Moon landing   16–17
ozone layer   18, 19
probes   20–21, 26–27
radio telescopes   8, 29
robots   26–27
satellites   4, 5, 18–19
shuttles   5, 13, 22–23
space race   14–15
space stations   5, 18, 24–25
spacesuits   12–13
space walks   14, 15
telescopes   5, 6–7, 8–9, 10, 14, 29

CREDITS AND NOTES

PICTURE AND ILLUSTRATION CREDITS

[t=top, b=bottom, l=left, r=right, c=centre, F=front, B=back, C=cover, bg=background]

AAP Image Library 24bl. **Julian Baum** 1c, 20bc. **Greg Bridges** 28–29c. **Tom Connell/Wildlife Art Ltd** 3tr, 5r, 12c, 17c, 18tl, 18tr, 19tl, 19tr, 22tl, 22tc, 23tl, 23tc, 23tr, 23cr, FCc. **Corel Corporation** 6br, 8tl, 19bc. **Digital Stock** 4bl, 5tl, 11tc, 14bl, 15tl, 15br, 22bc, 4–32 borders, Cbg. **Christer Eriksson** 28l, 31tr. **David A. Hardy/Wildlife Art Ltd** 2l, 10–11c, 21c, 21bl, 26l, FCtl. **MIX/NASA** 25cr, 25tl. **PhotoEssentials** 10bl, 16br, 17tc, 30bc. **The Photo Library/NASA/SPL** 13bl, 25cl. **Oliver Rennert** 6–7c, 9c. **Marco Sparaciari** 9tc, 29tr, BC. **Tony Wellington** 26–27br.

ACKNOWLEDGEMENTS

Weldon Owen would like to thank the following people for their assistance in the production of this book: Jocelyne Best, Peta Gorman, Tracey Jackson, Andrew Kelly, Sarah Mattern, Emily Wood.